THE
THREE
BIGGEST
LIES

THE THREE BIGGEST LIES

HOWARD SMITH

Illustrated by Bill Woodman

THE THREE BIGGEST LIES
A Bantam Book / December 1979

*Some excerpts originally appeared in "Scenes" by Howard Smith.
Reprinted by permission of* The Village Voice.
*Copyright © New Group Publications, Inc., 1979.
Illustrations by Bill Woodman.*

*All rights reserved.
Copyright © 1979 by Howard Smith.
This book may not be reproduced in whole or in part, by
mimeograph or any other means, without permission.
For information address: Bantam Books, Inc.*

ISBN 0-553-01209-3

Published simultaneously in the United States and Canada

Bantam Books are Published by Bantam Books, Inc.
Its trademark, consisting of the words "Bantam Books" and
the portrayal of a bantam, is registered in U.S. Patent and
Trademark Office and in other countries. Marca Registrada.
Bantam Books, Inc., 666 Fifth Avenue, New York, New York 10019.

PRINTED IN THE UNITED STATES OF AMERICA

0 9 8 7 6 5 4 3 2 1

The following friends made various contributions to this book, and I would like to thank them:

Bob and Rita Brand, Alexander Cockburn, Cathy Cox, Jane Gaynor, Linda Gillen, Linn Harris, John Hawkins, Sally Helgeson, Bill Levine, Jack Newfield, John Peecher, Meg Schneider, Debbie Solomon, John Stossel, Marilyn Surgil, Pam Sweeny, Brian and Wendy Van der Horst, Wendy Worth, Charles Yulish.

I would also like to thank the following people who originally contributed their lies to my "Scenes" column in the Village Voice, and who now see them, in whole or in part, here:

Shaun Considine, Marie Dippolito, F. Dole, Stanley Egelberg, Harold Hellman, Bruce and Joyce Levin Jacobs, Obin/Fields, Kevin Wadalavage, Stanley Weiser.

3 BIGGEST LIES:

1) Your check is in the mail.
2) Of course I can keep a secret.
3) I promise I'll only put it in a little way.

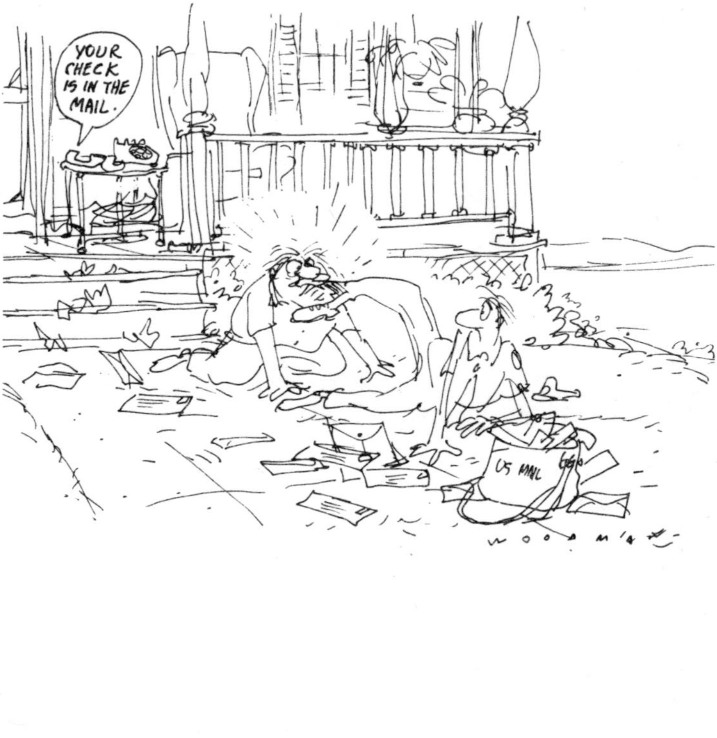
YOUR CHECK IS IN THE MAIL.
US MAIL

3 BIGGEST PRE-LIE LIES:

1) Would I lie to you?
2) I'm not clever enough to lie.
3) If I tried to lie, you'd see it in my face.

TAKING CARE OF BUSINESS

3 BIGGEST LANDLORD LIES:

1) Just tell us what you don't like about the apartment, and we'll have it all fixed up before you move in.
2) Don't worry about what it says in the lease; we'll always let you sublet.
3) This is definitely a very secure building; there's no way a robber can get in.

"Just tell us what you don't like about the apartment, and we'll have it all fixed up before you move in."

3 BIGGEST LIES
A STOCKBROKER TELLS
TO A NEW INVESTOR:

1) Owning a few shares of AT&T is just like owning a piece of America.

2) Let's face it, if I didn't do well for all my clients, I wouldn't still be in business.

3) Although I'm usually exceedingly conservative, I have an inside tip from the president of a certain big corporation that his stock is going to go right through the ceiling. However, we must move fast.

3 BIGGEST LIES A NEW INVESTOR TELLS TO HIS STOCKBROKER:

1) Look, I don't expect a quick killing, just a nice, steady, slow increase will make me happy, and . . .

2) Since you're the expert, I'll let you make all the decisions; however . . .

3) Just this morning I came across a sure thing. This guy who always eats breakfast with me at the same diner told me that his brother-in-law has a close friend who . . .

3 BIGGEST LIES YOU TELL THE IRS WHEN YOU FILE A VERY LATE RETURN:

1) I was out of the country around that time.
2) All my records got lost the last time I moved.
3) I thought my accountant took care of it.

INFLATION'S 3 BIGGEST LIES:

1) The curve is on the upswing, but it should level off in the next few months.
2) If you just do your part, we can lick this thing.
3) We're still better off than everyone else in the world.

3 BIGGEST MILLIONAIRE LIES:

1) Money isn't everything.
2) All of you are jealous that I'm so rich, but I'll bet none of you would like to pay my taxes.
3) Having inherited my family fortune is a responsibility that I take very seriously.

3 BIGGEST POOR MAN LIES:

1) I'd rather have peace of mind than be rich.
2) If I ever made a lot of money, I'd probably give it all away to my friends.
3) I'd keep right on working at this same job I've always had, even if I won the million-dollar lottery.

3 BIGGEST LIES FROM A BOWERY BUM:

1) I need some money so I can get something to eat; I won't spend it on booze.
2) I was once president of my own company and the guest of royalty.
3) Thanks, mister, I'll never forget your generosity.

3 BIGGEST PROSPECTIVE EMPLOYER LIES:

1) This company is very generous with raises.
2) We're all one big happy family.
3) Of course you'll never have to work overtime.

3 BIGGEST LAWYER LIES:

1) I won't charge you for this meeting.
2) Don't worry, I have the judge in my pocket.
3) If we have to go to trial, we'll win hands down in front of a jury.

3 BIGGEST LIES THE OFFICE XEROX MACHINE TELLS YOU:

1) I don't think that copy is too light to read.
2) I just had a new roll of paper put in this morning; I promise I won't run out in the middle of what you're doing.
3) Since I'm a marvel of space-age technology, it must be your fault I keep jamming.

MAY THE BEST MAN WIN

3 BIGGEST LIES BEFORE A GAME OF TENNIS:

1) Those lessons I took from Newcombe at tennis camp improved my serve one hundred percent.

2) This new Molybdenum Xyloflash Force X racquet gives me perfect control at the net.

3) I'm ready whenever you are. I never need much time to warm up.

"This new Molybdenum Xyloflash Force X racquet gives me perfect control at the net."

3 BIGGEST LIES DURING A GAME OF TENNIS:

1) I'm sure that net is high.
2) All those lobs of yours are at least two feet out.
3) Honestly, I wasn't aiming for your face.

3 BIGGEST LIES AFTER YOU'VE LOST A GAME OF TENNIS:

1) I'm glad you won. You deserved it. You played a great game.
2) The score would have been a lot closer if my new racquet had been more broken in.
3) I'm not really interested in the score just as long as I get a good workout.

3 BIGGEST KARATE LIES:

1) It's the beauty of movement that attracted me to this sport, not the aggression.
2) We don't have to weed out the psychopaths. It's amazing how passive really crazy people get after they learn to kill.
3) We're sorry that happened to you, but after all, you could have broken your hand while crossing the street.

3 BIGGEST KNICK MANAGEMENT LIES:

1) All we need is Spencer Haywood.
2) All we need is Bob McAdoo.
3) All we need is Marvin Webster.

3 BIGGEST RUNNING LIES:

1) Rain or shine, I always do five miles a day.
2) Boring? God no—it's one of the most exciting things I've ever done.
3) Remember, without pain, there can never be pleasure.

"Boring? God no—it's one of the most exciting things I've ever done."

DOCTOR FEELGOOD

3 BIGGEST HYPOCHONDRIAC LIES:

1) Up until now I've never been sick a day in my life.
2) None of the specialists I've been to can find anything wrong with me. . . . But what do they know?
3) I didn't do anything to deserve all this pain and trouble.

3 BIGGEST DOCTOR LIES:

1) If by tonight this doesn't clear up, just leave a message with my service and I'll get right back to you.
2) Talk to my assistant; he's just as good.
3) I'm just putting you into the hospital for an overnight checkup.

3 BIGGEST PSYCHIATRIST LIES:

1) If I didn't charge you such a high fee, you wouldn't take therapy seriously.
2) I would never sleep with a patient.
3) Of course I was listening.

3 BIGGEST LIES TOLD TO MENTAL HOSPITAL PATIENTS:

1) This is an "open" ward.
2) Sign the "voluntary" and you can get out whenever you want.
3) This injection will help you regain your own control.

3 BIGGEST CONTACT LENS LIES:

1) You know, without my glasses I'm actually quite good-looking.
2) I can see so much better, it was worth spending all that money.
3) Everyone down on your hands and knees; we'll find it in a second.

"Everyone down on your hands and knees; we'll find it in a second."

ALL YOU NEED IS LOVE

3 BIGGEST FALLING-IN-LOVE LIES:

1) At last! The real thing.
2) We're made for each other.
3) I'll never love anyone else.

3 BIGGEST LIES BOTH THE BOY AND THE GIRL ON A BLIND DATE TELL EACH OTHER:

1) You may not believe this, but I've never been on a blind date before.
2) Oh, any type of restaurant is okay with me. I eat all kinds of food.
3) We'll have to do this again sometime.

3 BIGGEST LIES A MAN USES TO PICK UP A WOMAN:

1) I never come to places like this and . . .
2) I've never talked to a strange woman before, but . . .
3) There's something about you that told me you were different.

"There's something about you that told me you were different."

3 BIGGEST LIES A WOMAN TELLS HERSELF TO LET HERSELF GET PICKED UP:

1) He doesn't look like he belongs in a place like this.

2) Oh well, at least really aggressive men are supposed to be great in bed.

3) At last! A guy who doesn't lie.

3 BIGGEST LIES FROM A FEMALE ONE-NIGHT STAND:

1) I don't normally do this on the first date.
2) That's okay, I like it that size.
3) It doesn't matter. I'll come next time.

3 BIGGEST LIES FROM A MALE ONE-NIGHT STAND:

1) I'll stop if you don't like it.
2) That's okay, I like them that size.
3) I'll call you Thursday night. Okay?

"I'll stop if you don't like it."

3 BIGGEST LIES AN EX-HUSBAND TELLS HIS EX-WIFE:

1) Of course you're still one of my best friends.

2) You'll be happy to know that the last weekend the kids slept over at my place, they related real great to my new girl friend, even though she's just a couple of years older than a teen-ager herself.

3) It must be the damn mails that held up my alimony check.

3 BIGGEST LIES AN EX-WIFE TELLS HER EX-HUSBAND:

1) It's hard for me to imagine that you and I were once married to each other.

2) At least this time I'm involved with a guy who isn't such a hopeless neurotic.

3) If you're late with the check one more time, I'll have you thrown in jail.

3 BIGGEST LIES ABOUT SEXUAL JEALOUSY:

1) Share and share alike, I've always said.
2) Jealousy is an infantile emotion and I've learned to completely transcend it.
3) You won't see me getting upset if you sleep with someone else, because what we have between us goes much deeper than sex.

PARENTAL GUIDANCE SUGGESTED

3 BIGGEST PARENT LIES:

1) This hurts us more than it hurts you.
2) We're only looking out for your best interests.
3) Someday you'll thank us.

3 BIGGEST LIES PARENTS TELL THEIR BABIES:

1) You're so cute. I don't mind getting up at five A.M.
2) Someday you'll grow up to be president.
3) I'll never do to you what my parents did to me.

3 BIGGEST LIES BABIES TELL THEIR PARENTS EVEN THOUGH THEY'RE STILL TOO YOUNG TO TALK:

1) I'll go right to sleep if you just nurse me a little longer.
2) I'll stop crying if you change my diaper.
3) Someday I'll grow up to be president.

3 BIGGEST CHRISTMAS LIES:

1) It always snowed on Christmas Eve when I was a kid.
2) It's the happiest time of the year.
3) It's better to give than receive.

3 BIGGEST LIES A WASP MOTHER TELLS HER DAUGHTER:

1) Our family came over on the *Mayflower*.
2) One of the most important things in life is to always remember your manners.
3) No daughter of mine is ever going to marry a Jew.

3 BIGGEST LIES A JEWISH MOTHER TELLS HER DAUGHTER:

1) The only man I'll ever let you marry is a nice Jewish doctor.
2) I'll get down on my hands and knees and scrub floors to get money to send you to Europe this summer.
3) You know what my problem is? I never complain.

3 BIGGEST LIES
KIDS TELL THEIR TEACHERS:

1) But I really do have to go to the bathroom.
2) My dog ate my homework.
3) I was late because my grandmother died.

3 BIGGEST LIES WHEN YOU
TAKE YOUR PARENT TO
A SENIOR CITIZENS HOME:

1) It's because we love you that we're bringing you here.
2) I'd like to spend some time at a place like this myself.
3) We'll come to visit you every Sunday.

FOLLOW THE LEADER

3 BIGGEST PRESIDENTIAL LIES:

1) "Prosperity is just around the corner."
2) "We are not going to send Americans in to do a job Asian boys can do."
3) "I am not a crook."

1. Herbert Hoover
2. Lyndon Johnson
3. Richard Nixon

3 BIGGEST LIES THE PENTAGON TELLS CONGRESS:

1) This new weapons system will cost no more than one billion dollars.

2) Because we made a few strategic design changes after the production mode had started, it's going to have a slight cost overrun of about twenty-five percent.

3) The sad truth, gentlemen, is that the project is going to cost three billion dollars because of the unions.

3 BIGGEST LIES OF A POLITICIAN RUNNING FOR OFFICE:

1) Above all else, I believe in being candid.

2) If elected, I'll fight for the working man.

3) If elected, I'll balance the budget and lower taxes.

3 BIGGEST LIES OF A POLITICIAN WHO HAS JUST LOST:

1) Even though I didn't win, I'm proud because we ran a clean campaign.

2) The *only* difference between me and my opponent was that he spent more money.

3) I guess American politics isn't ready for honesty.

3 BIGGEST LIES OF A POLITICIAN WHO HAS JUST WON:

1) Without my wonderful wife and terrffic kids, I couldn't have done it.

2) I see my win as a clear mandate to change the way our government has been run.

3) Just because my first appointee is my campaign manager doesn't mean he's not qualified for the job.

"Without my wonderful wife and terrific kids, I couldn't have done it."

3 BIGGEST SOUTH AMERICAN DICTATOR LIES:

1) To me, freedom of the press is one of the most cherished freedoms.

2) As soon as law and order is restored, we'll have free elections.

3) It is absolutely untrue that my opponents have been tortured and killed.

3 BIGGEST LIES COMMUNIST GOVERNMENTS TELL THEIR PEOPLE:

1) We have forged a truly classless society.

2) State ownership does not necessarily mean state control.

3) The reason we need such a large internal security apparatus is to keep our enemies out—not to keep you, our comrades, in.

3 BIGGEST LIES CAPITALIST GOVERNMENTS TELL THEIR PEOPLE:

1) The reason we need such a large internal security apparatus is because you can never trust a Commie.

2) In our free society, no matter what his humble beginnings, the poorest poor man can end up as the richest of the rich.

3) Socialism is one short step away from communism.

3 BIGGEST ESTABLISHMENT LIES:

1) Crime doesn't pay.
2) There's no such thing as a free lunch.
3) The best way to change things is to work within the system.

3 BIGGEST NEW YORK LIBERAL LIES:

1) The death penalty is no deterrant to murder.

2) Excessive welfare payments don't attract parasites to the city.

3) Open enrollment in the city colleges won't water down the diploma.

3 BIGGEST LIES OF THE LET'S-HAVE-ANOTHER-SUPERHIGHWAY LOBBY:

1) The studies prove that the only definite way to end traffic tie-ups, into and out of our city, is to build this new turnpike.

2) Putting up a new road always costs less than replacing the old one.

3) Once all the bondholders are paid back, we'll tear down the toll booths and make it a freeway.

3 BIGGEST LET'S-LEGALIZE-GAMBLING LIES:

1) It will drive the Mafia out of business.
2) It will reduce taxes.
3) It will stop police corruption.

3 BIGGEST LIES A REPORTER TELLS HIS SECRET SOURCE INSIDE CITY HALL:

1) I'm sure I can keep your name out of it.
2) Of course this is off the record.
3) I had nothing to do with that awful headline; the editor did it.

3 BIGGEST LIES VALEDICTORIANS USE IN THEIR GRADUATION SPEECH:

1) I can't tell you how much this diploma means to me.

2) Someday, we'll all look back on these high school years as the best of our lives.

3) Now we go forth prepared for all of life's crises.

ONLY ONE TO A CUSTOMER

3 BIGGEST DISCOUNT STORE LIES:

1) The price is three hundred dollars, complete.
2) We have one of the best service departments.
3) The only reason why that store across the street has it at a cheaper price is because they deal in stolen goods.

3 BIGGEST ADVERTISING LIES ABOUT A PRODUCT:

1) Tastes as good as homemade.
2) Last month my bust gained three inches.
3) Fast, *effective relief from the pain of hemorrhoidal tissue.

3 BIGGEST LIES YOU TELL YOURSELF BEFORE YOU BUY A PAIR OF VERY EXPENSIVE COWBOY BOOTS:

1) I look like Paul Newman.
2) I feel like Robert Redford.
3) I'm as tough as Clint Eastwood.

3 BIGGEST LIES A WOMAN IS TOLD AT A SHOE STORE:

1) My, what pretty feet.
2) Sure you can wear them in the rain.
3) Don't worry, they'll soften up in a day or two.

3 BIGGEST LIES A SALESMAN USES WHEN YOU'RE BUYING CLOTHES:

1) That will go well with absolutely any color.
2) Just take it to a tailor. A little work here and there and it will fit you like it was custom made.
3) That will never go out of style. It's a classic. You'll be wearing it for years.

"That will never go out of style. It's a classic. You'll be wearing it for years."

3 BIGGEST ANTIQUE STORE LIES:

1) It'll only cost you a couple of bucks to have it fixed.
2) I've never seen another one like it.
3) Next year I'll buy it back for twice the price.

"It'll only cost you a couple of bucks to have it fixed."

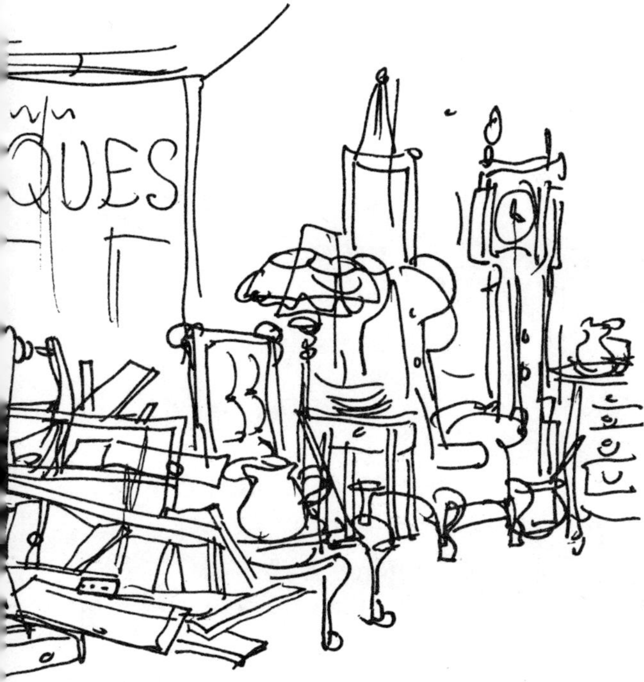
QUES

3 BIGGEST LIES YOUR BUTCHER USES WHEN SELLING YOU STEAK:

1) I weighed it after I trimmed the fat.
2) You'll be able to cut this with a butter knife.
3) Of course you'll find cheaper, but you'll never find better.

3 BIGGEST LIES YOUR GROCER USES WHEN SELLING YOU A MELON:

1) This baby is locally grown. It wasn't turned out in some greenhouse.
2) This beaut isn't too hard. It's absolutely guaranteed ready to eat tonight.
3) This gem only looks rotten. It's all dark and mushy because it's at the very peak of its ripeness.

3 BIGGEST HEALTH FOOD STORE LIES:

1) It tastes better without the sugar.
2) Once you've purified your system, you won't have those cravings anymore.
3) It comes all the way from the Hunza Mountains.

3 BIGGEST LIES YOU TELL YOUR PLANTS:

1) I'll replant you in a bigger pot tomorrow.
2) I'm sure enough light reaches you over here in this corner.
3) If you don't get flowers soon, I'm gonna feed you to the cats.

"You look like the type of person who'd be very good with plants."

3 BIGGEST LIES THEY TELL YOU IN A PLANT STORE:

1) You look like the type of person who'd be very good with plants.
2) You hardly ever have to water this one and it needs almost no light either.
3) Of course it'll have flowers.

3 BIGGEST LIES TOLD BY POT DEALERS:

1) It's pure Colombian.
2) It's pure Panamanian.
3) It's pure Hawaiian.

3 BIGGEST LIES TOLD BY COKE DEALERS:

1) This stuff is uncut.
2) Nobody else sells it this cheap.
3) I only deal to friends.

3 BIGGEST LIES BY A HIGH-PRICED HAIR STYLIST TO A WOMAN WHOSE LONG BEAUTIFUL TRESSES HE'S ITCHING TO CUT OFF:

1) None of the new clothes are designed to go with long hair any more.
2) It's the only way to get rid of broken ends.
3) Trust me. I'm the expert.

"Trust me. I'm the expert."

3 BIGGEST LIES
A NEW-CAR DEALER USES:

1) A few years from now when you trade this in for another one, it will hardly have depreciated at all.

2) With a *new* car, you'll just about never have to get it fixed.

3) I don't believe you're going to believe what that Commie jerk Ralph Nader said about this car.

3 BIGGEST LIES
A USED-CAR DEALER USES:

1) Someday this car will be a classic and sell for thousands of dollars.

2) This cream puff was owned by a little old lady who always kept it garaged.

3) We're honest. We've never turned the mileage back on a single car.

3 BIGGEST LIES A FOREIGN-CAR DEALER USES:

1) No need to worry about repairs and parts; we have dealers all over America.
2) Of course two kids can comfortably sit in the back.
3) There isn't a car on the road that gets as many miles per gallon as this one.

3 BIGGEST MECHANIC LIES:

1) We'll have the part tomorrow morning.
2) You'll have the car back by noon.
3) Of course it's covered by your warranty.

"No, no MSG."

3 BIGGEST CHINESE WAITER LIES:

1) No MSG.
2) No, no MSG.
3) You be okay.

3 BIGGEST CHINESE LAUNDRY LIES:

1) Definitely ready by Monday.
2) Those buttons were already broken before you brought the shirt in.
3) You didn't tell me no starch.

3 BIGGEST TOY STORE LIES:

1) It's unbreakable.
2) It's educational.
3) It's inexpensive.

IT'S ALL IN YOUR MIND

3 BIGGEST ENLIGHTENMENT LIES:

1) My guru has never lied to me.
2) I love every single human being.
3) You're the first person I've ever told my mantra to.

3 BIGGEST LIES ABOUT GETTING HIGH:

1) The only way I can listen to music is after I smoke a joint.
2) Sex isn't sex unless I'm stoned.
3) This is the highest I've ever been.

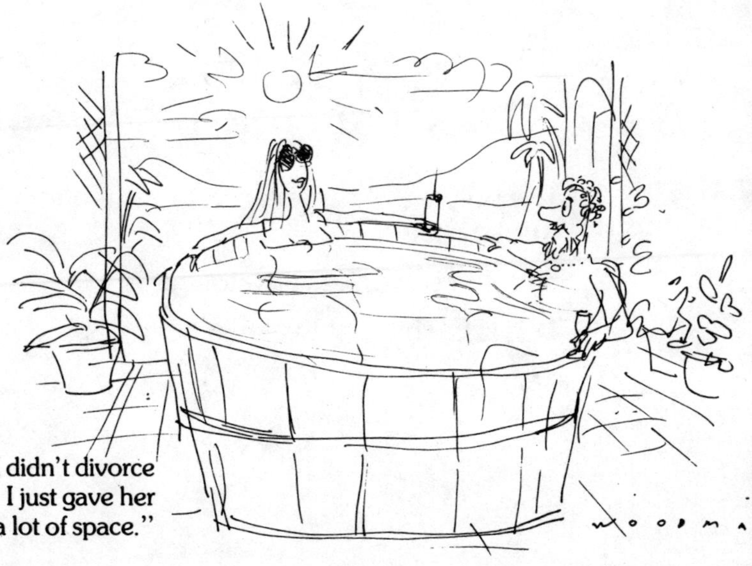

"I didn't divorce her. I just gave her a lot of space."

3 BIGGEST LIES BY AN EST GRADUATE:

1) I didn't divorce her. I just gave her a lot of space.
2) Werner doesn't have any money. He's given its context away.
3) I never speak in jargon. I'm just experiencing a share in your process to remake your agreements.

3 BIGGEST LIES PSYCHICS TELL:

1) Your palm is the most interesting I've seen.
2) You will meet a tall dark man and go on a long ocean voyage.
3) Of course seeing the future before it unfolds is expensive.

3 BIGGEST LIES OF AN OPTIMIST:

1) Things always have a way of working themselves out.
2) Well, at least it can't get any worse.
3) I can finally see the light at the end of the tunnel.

3 BIGGEST LIES OF AN PESSIMIST:

1) Where there's smoke there's fire.
2) You can't take it with you.
3) This is only the calm before the storm.

3 BIGGEST LIES ABOUT PYRAMID POWER:

1) Pyramids were brought to the desert by flying saucers from another planet.

2) All the secrets of the universe are hidden deep inside, if we could only decipher them.

3) The reason the dollar is so strong is because there's a drawing of a pyramid on one side.

WISH YOU WERE HERE

3 BIGGEST LIES BEFORE GOING TO LAS VEGAS:

1) I figured out an absolutely foolproof system to beat the house at blackjack.
2) I can just give myself a limit and I always stop if I lose.
3) Last time I was there I won a bundle.

3 BIGGEST LIES AFTER RETURNING FROM LAS VEGAS:

1) The entertainment gave me as big a thrill as the casinos.
2) If they hadn't changed the dealers on me I would have broken the bank.
3) I'll never gamble again.

3 BIGGEST LIES YOU TELL YOURSELF BEFORE MOVING TO NEW YORK CITY:

1) I'll be happier in a place where people keep their noses out of each other's business.

2) I'm going to see every Broadway show, go to the museums on Sunday, go to all the ballets, go to . . .

3) The next time you see me I'll be famous.

3 BIGGEST LIES YOU TELL PEOPLE IN NEW YORK ABOUT YOUR HOMETOWN:

1) Basically, I'm glad I grew up in a place where everyone knows each other.
2) You'd be surprised at all the well-known people who came from my town.
3) After I left, the whole area went downhill.

3 BIGGEST LIES YOU WRITE TO THE FOLKS BACK HOME:

1) I can get into Studio 54 anytime I want. I'm a regular.
2) Frank Sinatra and I live in the same building.
3) Underneath my glamorous life, I'm still just a small-town boy.

"Frank Sinatra and I live in the same building."

3 BIGGEST STEWARDESS LIES:

1) We are very glad to have you aboard.
2) Not only are we serving a really great dinner tonight but we'll also be showing a terrific film, Walt Disney's latest...
3) I'm sorry, sir, but we never go out with passengers so you'll have to stop annoying me.

3 BIGGEST AIRLINE PASSENGER LIES:

1) I bet I've flown so much that I've logged more miles than the pilot.
2) The only thing that makes me nervous about flying is the cab ride to the airport.
3) C'mon, honey, loosen up. I've gone out with a lot of you stews. You just want me to keep nagging so you can play hard to get.

3 BIGGEST AIRLINE PILOT LIES:

1) We appear to have run into some minor turbulence.
2) In a few minutes, if you all look out the windows on the right side of the plane, you'll get a clear view of the Grand Canyon.
3) There will be a slight delay while we circle the airport.

3 BIGGEST LIES AN AMERICAN IS TOLD IN ENGLAND:

1) Our weather isn't always this bad.
2) Once you get used to it, British food is actually quite good.
3) Our queen is a symbol we couldn't do without.

3 BIGGEST LIES AN AMERICAN IS TOLD IN FRANCE:

1) Everything sounds beautiful when it's spoken in French.
2) I don't know why you complain all the time about our telephones. We find they work just fine.
3) It is not true that for us French the world begins and ends with food.

3 BIGGEST LIES AN AMERICAN IS TOLD IN ITALY:

1) Our wines are just as good as the French.
2) This new coalition cabinet will last for years.
3) This kidnapping thing can't last forever.

3 BIGGEST LIES TOLD IN GERMANY WHEN ANYONE IS ASKED ABOUT WORLD WAR II:

1) I'm really Austrian.
2) I'm really Swiss.
3) In my little village we made only cameras. We knew nothing about the war until your planes bombed us.

FUR-LEGGED FRIENDS

3 BIGGEST LIES CATS TELL THEIR OWNERS:

1) Of course I won't run around all night and keep you up.

2) Don't worry about wearing black. I promise I won't leave hair around.

3) Are you kidding? I always use the litter box.

3 BIGGEST LIES DOGS TELL THEIR OWNERS:

1) This time I really will walk beside you if you let me off the leash.
2) I promise I won't drool if you let me put my head in your lap.
3) This is the last crotch I'll sniff.

"Don't worry about wearing black. I promise I won't leave hair around."

3 BIGGEST ZOO KEEPER LIES:

1) After a while, the animals don't notice the bars.

2) Big animals actually don't need as much exercise as you think.

3) The reason we don't want the public to feed the animals is that we give them a diet just like the one they ate out in the wild.

3 BIGGEST LIES ANIMALS IN THE ZOO TELL TO THE PUBLIC:

1) I'm very hungry. They hardly ever feed us here. Please throw me some peanuts before I starve to death.

2) We wouldn't fondle each other in plain view if we realized you'd get so embarrassed.

3) You can come closer. Would a cute little monkey like me pee on you?

THE SHOW MUST GO ON

3 BIGGEST LIES TOLD TO ACTORS AND ACTRESSES:

1) You did a wonderful reading; we'll get in touch with your agent.
2) I know we're paying way below scale, but all of you will get a percentage of the profits.
3) Honestly, you won't have to do a nude scene.

3 BIGGEST HOLLYWOOD FILM LIES:

1) Every cloud has a silver lining.
2) Everyone lives happily ever after.
3) The nicest guy always gets the most beautiful girl.

"A cowboy's hat never falls off."

3 BIGGEST WESTERN FILM LIES:

1) Horses are smart.
2) A cowboy's hat never falls off.
3) A six-gun fires at least twenty shots.

3 BIGGEST MUSICAL FILM LIES:

1) People dance on tables when they're happy.
2) People sing to each other when they're in love.
3) Very large orchestras can be hidden in very small places.

3 BIGGEST FOREIGN FILM LIES:

1) It's a great way to learn a foreign language.
2) Any man with an accent and a cigarette dangling from his lips is a great lover.
3) All women have lots of hair under their arms.

3 BIGGEST LIES BY A STAR GETTING AN ACADEMY AWARD:

1) I just want to say a few words.
2) I'm proud to work in an industry like ours.
3) I don't feel I really deserve this Oscar. I couldn't have done it without all the little people behind the scenes.

3 BIGGEST LIES FOLK SINGERS TELL:

1) I learned this next song from Woody.
2) I never play a tune the same way twice.
3) About the last thing I want to be is a commercial success.

3 BIGGEST LIES ROCK STARS TELL:

1) Dylan stole this song from me.
2) I haven't done a free concert because no one asked me.
3) I wish I could walk down the street without being recognized.

3 BIGGEST LIES ABOUT THE BEATLES:

1) A friend of mine in the music business says that next year the Beatles will definitely get together for one last concert.
2) Paul is dead.
3) Paul is alive.

3 BIGGEST COMEDIAN LIES:

1) Here's a joke I'm sure you've never heard, because...
2) The day you find me using somebody else's material will be a cold day in hell.
3) A funny thing happened to me on the way here tonight...

JOHNNY CARSON'S 3 BIGGEST LIES:

1) You're the best audience I've ever had.
2) I've never heard that joke before.
3) I'd like to introduce the next guest, one of my oldest and dearest friends.

HOWARD COSELL'S 3 BIGGEST TELEVISION LIES:

1) Standing next to me is an athlete who's the greatest living legend of our time...

2) Standing next to me is an incredible athlete who is the most tremendous credit to his chosen profession...

2) Standing next to me is a man who is more than a mere athlete, he is a paragon among paragons, a hero among heroes, a gladiator among gladiators...

"Standing next to me..."

PUTTING YOUR BEST FOOT FORWARD

3 BIGGEST OOPS-I-JUST-FARTED LIES:

1) This chair is sure squeaky.
2) I'm very hot; could we open a window?
3) Excuse me, but I have to leave right this second or I'll be late for an appointment I just remembered.

3 BIGGEST YOU'RE-TALKING-ON-THE-PHONE-AND-HAVE-TO-GO-TO-THE-BATHROOM LIES:

1) There's someone at the door; could I call you right back?
2) I've got something boiling over on the stove. I'll call you right back.
3) No, no. I'm listening to you.

"No, no, I'm listening to you."

3 BIGGEST LIES WHEN CAUGHT PICKING YOUR NOSE:

1) I was just scratching my lip.
2) I was just scratching my eye.
3) I did it to see if you were paying attention.

3 BIGGEST I'M-NOT-UPSET-THEY-FIRED-ME LIES:

1) I was overqualified to begin with.
2) I bet they'll have to replace me with two people.
3) I really quit.

3 BIGGEST LIES ABOUT A FAT WOMAN:

1) If she didn't wear those gaudy clothes, she wouldn't look so huge.
2) She's got big bones so she carries it really well.
3) She's got such a pretty face.

3 BIGGEST LIES ABOUT A FAT MAN:

1) There's a guy who's never seen the tops of his shoes.
2) I'll bet he's strong as a bull.
3) He's got such a great sense of humor—he's always laughing.

3 BIGGEST LIES SHORT PEOPLE TELL TALL PEOPLE:

1) Good things come in small packages.
2) Some of the greatest heroes in history were short.
3) When most tall women dance with a guy my size, they don't even notice the difference.

3 BIGGEST LIES TALL PEOPLE TELL SHORT PEOPLE:

1) Of course I understand what it's like being short. There was a time in my life when I was short for my age too.

2) Believe me, I'd be happy to be as short as you. At least I'd be able to find clothes that fit.

3) The only reason you hate me is because I'm so much taller than you.

"When most tall women dance with a guy my size, they don't even notice the difference."

3 BIGGEST MEMORY LIES:

1) I've never lost my keys before.
2) You have a face I'll always remember.
3) I'll never forget what's-his-name.

3 BIGGEST LIES ABOUT LYING:

1) A little white lie never hurt anyone.
2) What you don't know won't hurt you.
3) The truth shall set you free.

ATTENTION LIARS

I'm glad you enjoyed reading this collection, but I know you think you could have done better. Here's your chance. Since we might do a sequel to this book I would like to invite you to send in your own lines. What subject? Anything at all—don't feel limited by the categories covered in this book.

Please Mail Them To:

> Smithbrand
> P.O. Box 275
> Cooper Station
> New York, N.Y. 10003

For those of you who are seeking fame and fortune, seek elsewhere. You will not be reimbursed. All contributions whether or not published, become my property, and nothing you send can be returned. That's what you deserve for being such a big liar. Or are you? Unless you Pinocchios waste a fifteen cent stamp you'll never have the satisfaction of letting me know that your nose is really as long as you claim.

ABOUT THE AUTHOR

HOWARD SMITH has been the writer of the weekly "Scenes" column in the *Village Voice* since 1966, during which time he also originated and wrote, for three years, the "Playboy Sex Polls" column. In the early seventies he had his own rock music and interview show on WPLJ, plus a taped program syndicated to radio stations around the country. Mr. Smith produced and directed *Marjoe* for which he won the academy award for Best Documentary feature in 1973, and *Gizmo*, his most recent feature film which he also produced and directed, will open this summer.

ABOUT THE ILLUSTRATOR

BILL WOODMAN is a free-lance cartoonist and illustrator whose work has appeared in many national magazines including the *New Yorker, Playboy, National Lampoon,* and *Esquire*.